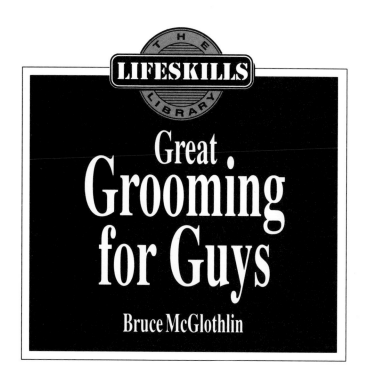

THE LIFESKILLS LIBRARY

Great
Grooming
for Guys

Bruce McGlothlin

THE ROSEN PUBLISHING GROUP, INC.
NEW YORK

Published in 1993 by The Rosen Publishing Group, Inc.
29 East 21st Street, New York, NY 10010

First Edition
Copyright 1993 by The Rosen Publishing Group, Inc.

Manufactured in the United States of America

Library of Congress Cataloging-in-Publication Data

McGlothlin, Bruce.
     Great grooming for guys / Bruce McGlothlin.—1st ed.
        p.   cm. — (The Life skills library)
     Includes bibliographical references and index.
     Summary: Offers practical advice on such topics as personal cleanliness, health, diet, exercise, and clothes.
     ISBN 0-8239-1468-2
     1. Grooming for boys—Juvenile literature. [1. Grooming.] I. Title
II. Series.
RA777.2.M36 1993
646.7'044—dc20
                                      92-39619
                                         CIP
                                         AC

CONTENTS

INTRODUCTION

Mark is 15, and about to start his sophomore year in high school. In the past few years he has begun to realize that he is losing his friends. A pattern is developing, and now Mark is getting worried.

What is wrong with Mark? How did this happen to him? Let's take a closer look.

To begin with, Mark is dirty. There is always grime under his fingernails. His hair is long, greasy, and unkempt. Pimples cover his face. He has a bad habit of picking at them, and his skin is beginning to show scarring.

Mark wears the same clothes for days. You can tell by his body odor that showers are not a high priority with him. His jeans are torn and stained. His shirt is wrinkled and hangs out. His sneakers are worn and caked with dirt. He says that he wants to be comfortable.

Impressing others is important to Mark. To show how grown-up he is, he has begun to smoke cigarettes and drink beer. Both make him sick, but he won't admit that. Now the smell of cigarettes also fills his clothes. Brushing his teeth is too much trouble, so he also has bad breath. Mark has been suspended from school several times for smoking and drinking. Most of his schoolmates think he is a druggie, but he has not used hard drugs yet.

Mark has gained a lot of weight because he eats so much junk food. He used to participate in sports, but he no longer has the energy.

Although Mark is intelligent, his grades are very low. Mark's home life is very unhappy. His parents are divorced. He lives with his mother and sees his father only on weekends. He shows his anger at both of his parents by disobeying them constantly. He is so frustrated by the way his life is going that he is considering quitting school altogether. He especially resents the efforts of his parents and school officials to get him into counseling.

Mark has also become a bully, threatening and beating up younger children. Other kids say he has "a chip on his shoulder."

Mark realizes that something is wrong. He hopes he can find a way to change.

Let's see how good grooming habits and positive self-esteem can help Mark become the person he would like to be.

WHAT IS GOOD GROOMING?

You have probably known about good grooming since you were very young, but you never did it yourself. Your mother or father bathed and dressed you. Being neat and clean was a parent's responsibility then. Eventually, however, you began to look after yourself.

But some kids are never taught these good habits. Some parents pay no attention to grooming. Thus, their children learn their bad habits.

On the other hand, some parents overemphasize the idea of cleanliness and neatness. When the kids reach middle- and high-school age they may rebel. Being sloppy and dirty can become "their thing."

Probably you learned the basics of good grooming from your parents or other adults. But you

—

Good grooming helps to create a positive self-image.

gradually begin to watch what your peers do, what they say, and how they act. You notice clothes and fashions in particular. Athletes and television or movie stars may become role models for you. Some may be good role models, others may not. But kids want to be with the "in crowd."

Your primary goal is to be liked by others. You pay attention to what others say about you. If you sense negative reactions, you may change your ways. But positive acceptance will convince you that you are doing the "right" things.

When you reach the middle- or high-school years, you are responsible for your own grooming and appearance. Whether you receive positive or negative comments rests entirely on your shoulders. Parents and teachers can only act as advisers.

More Than Looking Good

Many people think good grooming is the same as personal hygiene. But it is much more than being neat and clean and wearing the right clothes. Good grooming is a lifetime "attitude" of making positive choices that will increase your self-esteem. You can start by developing good habits for your body.

You need to maintain physical fitness all your life. Fitness can be fun. If it becomes a chore, quitting will be too easy. Fitness can make life more enjoyable. Exercise and sports should be part of it.

Everyone is concerned about diet these days. It is important to watch not only the kinds of food we eat, but also the quantity. With poor food choices and little exercise, you will gain weight. Being careful of your diet is an important part of a positive self-image.

The dangers of alcohol, tobacco, and other drugs are well known today. Don't let yourself be pressured into trying them. The use of stimulants and depressants can shorten your life.

Grooming deals with the body first. A tasteful appearance projects a positive self-image. But there is also a behavioral side. How you relate to others in social situations is critical to good grooming.

The Difference Good Grooming Makes

When you feel neat, clean, and attractive, other people notice. They sense your high degree of self-esteem and confidence.

Your personal appearance carries over to your schoolwork. You may not be aware of it, but it happens. You radiate an air of satisfaction and belief in yourself that goes beyond appearance.

People will notice you. They will smile and look at you more closely. They will think good thoughts about you. Peers, teachers, parents, and employers will make positive judgments about you.

When you receive approval for your appearance and attitude toward others, your self-esteem increases. You gain people's trust. Others listen to you and want to be with you. They may begin seeing you as a positive role model.

Making a Commitment to Positive Action

Look at yourself in the mirror. Don't pull any punches. How do you look right now? What do you like about your grooming and behavior?

What about the negative habits that you would like to change? Make a list of them. Develop some plans that are possible to carry out. Work on only one or two things at a time. Make gradual changes that you can live with, and watch how quickly they become habits.

The Value of Good Grooming

Studies by experts show that people who have pride in themselves and their abilities tend to attract other people. They are interesting to their friends and family. They tend to be copied by others. In turn, being highly regarded increases their self-esteem.

Do you want to be in that position? Do you want to be seen positively by your friends and adults? Do you want greater self-esteem?

In the chapters ahead good grooming is discussed in more detail. As you read, think about Mark. Try to imagine how others see him. What positive changes do you think he could make?

Compare Mark to yourself. Do you have any of his habits? What will you do to make the necessary changes.

PERSONAL HYGIENE

Personal hygiene is the care and cleanliness of the body and its parts. When the human body is dirty, it produces an unpleasant odor that can turn others away. It is commonly known as body odor, or B.O. Just imagine being trapped in an elevator with ten football players who have just finished a practice session.

When you are very active, your body releases a fluid to help you cool down. That fluid, which is called sweat, also contains waste materials. If the sweat dries on your skin or clothes, it becomes B.O.

But did you know that you sweat all the time, even as you sit reading this book? The body is constantly releasing waste materials through the pores of the skin.

So you can see why it is important to take a shower or a bath at least once a day. Most men prefer showers, to wash the dirt and sweat down the drain. A shower also gives the skin a gentle massage and makes you feel more alert.

Using soap and a washcloth or sponge is a must. Some people like to use a loofah sponge. Loofah is made from a dried vine. It is quite rough and scrubs away dead skin. After rubbing the loofah sponge on your body, rinse thoroughly from head to toe.

Dry all body parts with a large, soft towel. This also helps to increase circulation and makes your skin feel warm and glowing.

Now that you are thoroughly clean, have you finished? Not quite. It is important to remember to use a deodorant every day. Most B.O. comes from the armpits, and a deodorant provides extra protection. You may choose a roll-on, stick, or spray type.

After a shower, always put on clean underwear and socks. You don't want any soiled clothes next to your clean body.

Hair

Your hair is one of the first things that people notice about you. Some people like to make a "statement" by wearing their hair wild and outlandish. Others are more conservative and follow current styles. But your hairstyle really doesn't matter, as long as it is neat and clean.

———

Regular showers are an important part of daily grooming.

Some people's hair tends to be oily, others, dry. Look at your own hair and scalp. Which type is yours? How often do you need to wash it to keep it clean and manageable? You must decide whether it needs to be washed every day or once a week.

A good shampoo removes oil and dust. Be sure to massage the shampoo well into your scalp to provide extra circulation. Rinse thoroughly to remove all shampoo. Dry your hair roughly with a towel. Finish with a hair dryer if you like.

At times you may develop dandruff or a scaly scalp that makes your hair look messy and unkempt. Flakes may appear on dark-colored shirts or jackets. If you notice this, buy a medicated shampoo, which should clear up the dandruff in a short time.

Combing your hair several times a day adds to its overall neatness and manageability. It is important to wash your comb and brush regularly with warm soapy water. It is best not to use another person's comb or brush. That can pass germs and disease to your scalp.

Skin

As you move into the teenage years, you may have noticed that your skin is oily by the end of the day. This is natural. However, oily skin may become more of a problem if you eat junk foods that are high in fat, such as cake, cookies, and potato chips. Also, your body is undergoing changes that increase the oils in your skin.

As a teenager you are probably very active. Activity increases the chances for dirt to collect in the pores of your skin. With the build-up of oil and dirt come pimples and blackheads.

What is the first thing to do for a pimple? Don't pick at it! That can lead to scarring, which will never go away.

If you notice pimples or blackheads, wash your face with soap and water frequently. That means two or three times a day—more, if possible. Remember that *acne* is caused by dirt and oil build-up. If you are still having a problem, consider using a medicated soap, cream, or pad. Also, watch your diet and cut back on oily or greasy foods.

If your skin does not improve, you may want to consult a *dermatologist*, a doctor who specializes in treating skin problems.

Shaving

By now you have probably noticed some growth of hair on your face. This is called stubble or a beard. It is a sign that you are rapidly reaching manhood. When the growth begins to be heavy, it is time to think about shaving.

You can decide whether to use an ordinary razor and shaving cream or an electric razor. Try both and see which you prefer.

In school or other public places, it is important to be clean-shaven. People will notice an unshaven face. It may "say" unfavorable things about you.

Many men today wear beards or mustaches. This may appeal to you as a way to be like a brother or father or other role model. But it may take some time for your beard to grow long enough to wear this style. Also, some schools and jobs do not permit facial hair. It is probably best for teenagers to shave daily.

Many men enjoy using an aftershave lotion. This feels good and smells good, but it is not essential. If you do use an aftershave, don't overdo it. Just a drop or two will do the job.

Fingernails

Your hands are involved in many activities, from shuffling papers to changing the oil in the car. They are always exposed to dirt, which will surely find its way under the fingernails.

It is a good idea to wash your hands several times a day, and especially after using the toilet. Fingernails should be scrubbed with a small brush and soap. A nail file and manicure scissors or nail clipper will help to remove dirt and keep your nails well shaped.

Nails should be trimmed weekly. The *cuticle,* or skin around the nail bed, should also be trimmed if possible.

If your occupation involves constant use of your hands and exposes them to dirt, you must work extra hard to maintain high standards of cleanliness.

—

Some basic grooming items are helpful to maintain personal hygiene.

Those are some of the thoughts that occur to other kids when they look at you.

Your clothes should be comfortable and give you a sense of self-confidence. When people compliment you about your clothes, it makes you feel good. When others criticize, it makes you stop and think. If you need help in choosing the right clothes, be attentive to what people may say.

Look around for positive role models at school, at home, or in the neighborhood. What kind of comments are made about their clothes? Do you want to receive the same reaction?

Let's look at some tips that may help you to plan your wardrobe.

Seasonal Wear

Planning your wardrobe will depend a great deal on the climate where you live. The main idea is to dress comfortably and suitably for various weather conditions.

In spring and summer people wear looser and lighter-weight clothes such as short-sleeved shirts, shorts, and sport coats. Cotton is a particularly cool, comfortable, and casual fabric for the warm months of the year. Many young men wear cotton all year round because of its pleasant feel. You may need several layers to be warm enough in cooler temperatures.

Clothing will last longer and look better when properly cared for.

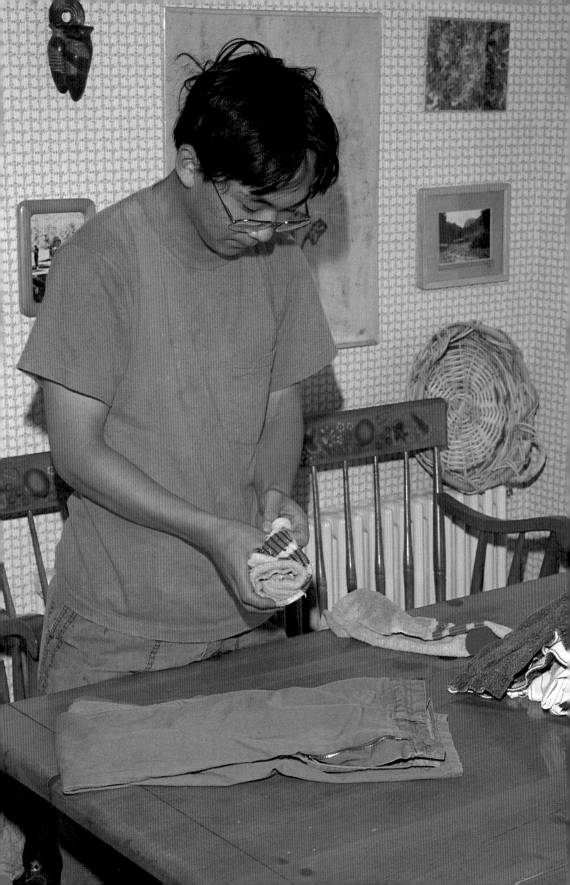

Fall and winter weather requires heavier clothing. Long-sleeved shirts, sweaters, and corduroy or wool pants provide warmth against wintry temperatures.

Choosing Colors and Patterns

Ask yourself what kind of appearance you want to make. Remember, first you want to dress comfortably. Then you want to make a good impression on others.

You need to choose clothes that look well on you and coordinate together. Wearing checked pants, a plaid shirt, and a striped tie may be comfortable, but it will probably get you laughed at. Checks or plaids should be worn with solid colors.

The same careful taste applies to colors. Bright red, orange, or yellow attract attention. They are best worn to parties or other social occasions.

The more conservative colors such as blue, green, pink, purple, beige, or gray tend to be easier on the eyes. They suggest that you want to be considered more quiet and reserved but tasteful in appearance. They are better received at job interviews and more serious occasions.

There may be times when you want to be noticed and other times when you prefer to remain in the background. Try both kinds of colors and observe the reactions of others. Which reflects the type of person you want to be?

—

Choosing solid colors to go with plaids or stripes will make a more coordinated outfit.

Special Occasions

As you get older, you will discover that special occasions require specific types of clothing. Look ahead to the near future. Are you planning to attend a prom, dance, or party? What will you wear? Do you own the right kind of outfit? Will you have to buy something new?

A prom usually requires more formal dress. For men, "formal" usually means a tuxedo. Most men don't own a tuxedo. You can rent a tuxedo from a specialty clothing store. Usually there are many styles and colors to choose from.

Dressing in a tuxedo for the first time is quite an experience. You will probably need help from a parent or other adult.

Parties and dances may be formal or semiformal, which means a coat-and-tie affair. Parties may also be casual, so it is important to find out in advance what attire is expected. Showing up in the wrong clothing could be embarrassing.

Casual attire means comfortable, simple, everyday clothing—but it also means neat and clean. Your friends will still make judgments about you in your casual clothes.

When you go for a job interview, wear clothes appropriate for the type of work you might be doing. For any kind of office job, wear a suit. If you are applying for a job picking apples in an orchard, you can wear jeans and a pullover top. But always be clean and neat.

Shopping for Clothes

Up to now you may never have shopped alone for your own clothes.

By starting to shop for yourself, you can begin to decide what you like and what you don't like. You can establish a style for yourself.

But where do you shop? In a department store, a clothing store, a discount store? This decision usually depends on how much money you have. Now is the time to become a smart shopper.

When starting out, you will probably learn by trial and error. Some things you buy may look good at first but will tear or fade after only a few washings. You will become alert to the quality of certain fabrics and manufacturers. Be prepared to spend a little more to get good quality.

Be a good shopper and look around for what is the best value. Try the garment on to see how it fits and how it looks on you. Be sure to save the sales receipt in case you need to return it.

Clothes are expensive. Always think about what you already own before you buy anything new. Mixing and matching your wardrobe can stretch your clothing budget.

Maintaining Your Wardrobe

As you begin to choose your own wardrobe, it is also important to maintain it. That means keeping it neat, clean, and pressed. Pants, shirts, socks, and

underwear should be washed often. Sweaters and sports jackets should be sent to the dry cleaner.

Once a year, go through your complete wardrobe. See what is too small, what is in need of repair, and what you are simply tired of. Clothes that you have outgrown or won't wear again might be welcomed by a younger relative or friend. Or you might send them to one of the organizations that collect clothing for the poor or homeless.

Footwear

Shoes are an important part of your wardrobe, too. They are as important to your health as to your style. Be sure new shoes fit properly and are comfortable when you try them on.

Most teenagers love sneakers and wear them just about everywhere. Unfortunately, some sneakers have become a status symbol, and many kids think that they must pay exorbitant amounts of money for a brand name. Good sneakers don't have to be very expensive. Shop around.

You should have one or two pairs of leather shoes for dress or casual occasions. Keeping your shoes well polished will make them wear longer. Pay attention to signs of wear in your shoes. Dress shoes can be resoled or be given new heels and look almost like new. Wearing worn-out shoes will make you look sloppy and can damage your feet.

—

It is wise to examine clothes for workmanship and durable fabrics as well as style.

FITNESS

Here are four statements about physical fitness. Which are true?

- Fitness is fun.
- Fitness is easy.
- Fitness helps to develop an attractive body.
- Fitness is relaxing.

If you said all four statements are true, you are right. They can all be true for you if you make fitness part of your everyday life.

However, most of us say we are too busy. We have become experts in making excuses for not exercising. "I have no one to go with." "I'll start tomorrow." "I don't have time."

As a result, we tend to eat more and gain weight. Our heart does not pump enough blood through

Exercising on a regular basis will help you feel and look better.

our body. Cholesterol builds up fatty deposits in our blood vessels. We get headaches from the stress of everyday living. We feel bad and look even worse. Our self-esteem takes a nose-dive. Then we begin to feel guilty about our appearance.

If that sounds like you, go look at yourself in the mirror. How do you look? More important, how do you feel? Perhaps it is time to pay closer attention to your level of physical fitness.

A fitness routine does many good things for the body. It increases the chemicals called *endorphins*, which increase relaxation. It lowers the fat level and replaces it with muscle. More blood is pumped to all parts of the body. The oxygen level in the brain is increased, which is believed to increase creativity. And it plays a role in preventing illness.

It may surprise you to know that exercise increases rather than decreases energy levels. You can do more without becoming fatigued. You sleep better at night and feel more rested in the morning.

As you can see, fitness can bring many benefits to the physical body. It also brings many benefits to your psychological self. When you look well and feel well, you feel better about yourself. You develop super self-esteem.

Choosing a Type of Exercise

Many different types of exercise can be used to achieve physical fitness. Team sports are popular, and those who are successful at a particular game may receive a great deal of public attention. Some parents pressure teenagers to compete in sports such as football, basketball, and baseball to satisfy some need of their own. But the sport you choose should be right for you, not for someone else. A 5'2", 92-pound boy probably will not make the football team but may be a whiz at cross-country running. On the other hand, a heavier, muscular type might be good at football but lack the speed and endurance required for track-and-field events.

You may want to experiment with both team and individual sports in school. Team sports require cooperation and interaction. Individual sports tend to develop personal skills, self-motivation, and self-discipline. All sports teach physical coordination.

Let's look at the three body types and see what sports or fitness activities might suit them.

The *ectomorphic* body type is lean and tall with long limbs. People with this body build tend to do well at basketball, baseball, soccer, lacrosse, track, bicycling, and tennis.

The *endomorphic* body type is softer and more rounded, or pear-shaped. People with this body build tend to have more body fat and to be slower in nature. They may like sports in which they can use their whole body weight, such as football, wrestling, and hockey.

The *mesomorphic* body type is more muscular and athletic. People with this body build may enjoy a variety of energetic sports such as swimming, football, volleyball, weight lifting, or hockey.

High school offers many opportunities to participate in team sports and compete within the school and with other schools. Training and discipline are required at this level of competition. Some teens thrive on such demands and develop in the areas of strength, speed, coordination, and team play.

Other young people are not as competitive. They may prefer sports that offer more personal satisfaction such as tennis, swimming, gymnastics, golf, running, skiing, or archery.

Physical Advantages of Exercise

Your life can be better in many ways from exercise. Let's look at the physical benefits.

• With any physical activity, your heart pumps more blood to various parts of the body. This not only increases the strength of the various organs, but strengthens the heart itself. Blood vessels—the arteries and veins—increase in size to allow more blood to flow to and from the heart. More capillaries, the tiny blood vessels that connect the arteries and veins, are created.

• Regular exercise helps in maintaining a proper body weight. Your appearance improves. Exercise is especially important if you try to lose weight. Fat will change to muscle.

• The body becomes much stronger and better able to fight off illness and disease. Exercise helps

---

Relaxation and a healthy snack can be part of the daily routine.

to raise body temperature, which in turn can assist in killing germs and viruses that enter the body.

• Exercise helps to create higher levels of "good cholesterol." This helps to fight the "bad cholesterol" that clogs arteries with fatty deposits. When arteries are clogged the blood supply is cut off, and a heart attack may occur.

• Endurance levels increase, providing more energy during the course of the day.

• The body releases more of the chemicals called endorphins. These substances are natural painkillers and relaxants and help to improve one's mood.

Psychological Advantages of Exercise

Exercise can do wonderful things for your state of mind.

• As your physical condition improves, your self-esteem rises. High self-esteem helps you to handle problems and stress better.

• As you push yourself to maintain your schedule of exercise, you become more committed and self-disciplined. In fact, you may feel guilty if you miss a session.

• Your outlook on life becomes somewhat more relaxed. You may not become upset so easily. Patience enables you to cope with difficult situations.

• Negative thoughts and ideas can be handled in a more positive way. You can begin to look on the bright side of things. You may also be less critical of others.

DIET

Food and water are the basic necessities of life. If we eat and drink properly, it helps our body to grow and become stronger.

As a child, you probably received good nutrition by eating what your parents provided for you. As you grow older, it is time to learn what foods are healthful and what foods are to be avoided.

Candy and other sweet foods and beverages provide quick energy. But they also contain large amounts of sugar and fat. They provide nothing good except the quick energy. And they add unwanted pounds.

A lifetime goal should be to eat a healthful diet, with a strong emphasis on fruits and vegetables. Remember, too, that diet and exercise go hand in hand in maintaining a good body image. And a good body image promotes high self-esteem.

Food Groups

The foods that we eat are made up of proteins, carbohydrates, fats, and liquids. All of these foods contain a variety of vitamins and minerals that are needed for a healthy body. Water is the liquid that is essential to the body.

Here are some examples of each food group.

- Proteins: Eggs, fish, meat, milk products, nuts, potatoes, whole grain cereals.
- Carbohydrates: Cereals, fruits, potatoes, sugar, pasta.
- Fats: Animal fat, milk products, nuts, oils.
- Vitamins: Eggs, fish, fruits, vegetables, milk, milk products, nuts, whole grain cereals, yeast.
- Minerals: Cereals, eggs, fish, fruits, meat, milk products, nuts, vegetables, yeast.
- Liquids: Water, milk, fruits, vegetables.

There is a wide variety of foods that can help you grow and develop a healthy body. If you eat a well-balanced diet of these foods, you will probably get all the vitamins and minerals your body needs.

Obesity

Obesity simply means being too fat. Obese people may not look well in their clothes. Their weight hampers their activity. They tend to have very low self-esteem.

—

Eating well-balanced meals is important for good health and a wholesome appearance.

Obesity is not common among teenagers. But being slightly overweight may be a warning that you need to exercise more and watch your diet.

Dieting

Dieting has become a *fad* in our society. But it is a fad that can be dangerous to your health. Teens, especially girls, have become so obsessed with being thin that they often diet themselves into eating disorders such as *anorexia nervosa* and *bulimia*.

For a diet to be healthful and successful, it must meet three conditions. First, it must be reasonable and sensible. That means eating the right kinds of food in the proper proportions. If you must snack, choose raw vegetables and fruit.

The second condition is that the diet must be accompanied by regular exercise. That means working out 30 to 40 minutes 3 to 5 times a week. Your goal is to turn the stored fat into muscle. You can do that through exercise.

The third condition is to develop the self-discipline to maintain the first two conditions. It may help to participate in a group for support, but at some point you need to do it for yourself.

People who go on diets talk a great deal about vitamins and special food supplements. Generally most of the vitamins and minerals you need are contained in a healthful diet.

There is no secret about dieting. It is just common sense and sticking to the three conditions.

GROOMING YOUR SELF-ESTEEM

The grooming of one's personality is a key factor in achieving overall good grooming. Parts of the personality are the behaviors (actions) and attitudes that promote self-esteem. Self-esteem means how you perceive yourself, but it also includes how you behave toward yourself and others.

People with high self-esteem do things in a positive manner. They are upbeat about themselves and their world. They show positive attitudes toward others and refuse to be influenced by negative people. They tend to be happy and, by the same token, popular.

On the other hand, people with low self-esteem constantly focus on doom and gloom. They seldom are able to see the bright side of anything. They are very good at criticizing others. But underneath is usually strong doubt about themselves.

Let's review some of the actions of people with high self-esteem. These ways of behaving are an important part of good grooming skills.

Self-Control

Life today is filled with many pressures. They come from parents, teachers, and peers. And they can cause extreme nervousness or anxiety.

When anxiety becomes high, teenagers are likely to become upset and lose control of their emotions. They may resort to pushing, shoving, and shouting. A person with high self-esteem may have the ability to maintain control in stressful situations.

How would you describe yourself? What do you do when things get tough? Do you stay calm and try to think clearly, or do you tend to blow up and strike out at everyone around you?

Maintaining self-control can take a lot of practice. Start by trying to focus on positive things. Let minor annoyances pass.

At times it may seem that you cannot hold your emotions in check without striking back. But you may be surprised at how much control you actually have. Tell yourself to remain calm. Take a deep breath. Count to ten slowly. Remember, no one can make you lose control except yourself.

——

Showing consideration for people around you will add to your self-esteem.

Assertiveness

Assertiveness is an attitude of confidence and self-assurance. It suggests that you have respect for yourself and will stand up for your rights.

Assertiveness is not showing disrespect for others. You respect yourself enough, however, to speak your mind honestly. That sometimes takes a great deal of courage.

Do you speak up when you know a wrong has been done? If you do try to correct the situation, you are acting assertively.

Assertiveness is not aggressiveness. Aggressive behavior shows a lack of respect for others and a willingness to resort to verbal or physical violence. Assertive behavior, on the other hand, shows a sense of self-respect and a willingness to stand up for what one thinks is right.

Few of us are born with assertiveness. It needs to be practiced over and over. It also requires belief in oneself. With practice, however, it can become easier.

Manners

One of the most obvious traits of people with high self-esteem is good manners. Manners involve a basic knowledge and understanding of how to treat other people.

Do you demonstrate good manners in your every-day behavior? Do you customarily remember to say

"Please," "Thank you," and "Excuse me"? Little acts of politeness such as holding a door say a lot about your respect for others.

Consideration for Yourself

While we are stressing the importance of consideration for others, we must not overlook the need to be considerate of yourself.

At times you are bound to be in situations and relationships that are frustrating and negative. It can become easy to blame yourself.

When you feel like a failure, try focusing on your positive traits. Be good to yourself.

Treat yourself to the little rewards and pleasures that make life worth living. Go for a walk. Read a book. Visit a friend. Play a favorite tape.

Having a bad day is nothing to be ashamed of. You may just need some time to think and relax.

Part of successful living is being involved with others. People tend to talk about their interests. Your job is to become a good listener. And if you ask questions about the thoughts and opinions of others, you can learn a lot, too. Treat yourself and others with respect and concern. You will be rewarded again and again for your positive attitude.

PUTTING IT ALL TOGETHER

In the Introduction, we considered the sad case of Mark, who had lost most of his friends and found his self-esteem going way down.

Mark, however, was beginning to realize that something was wrong. He really didn't want to be the kind of person he had become. And he decided to do something about it.

To begin with, Mark resolved to be clean. He began to shower daily and take care of his body. He has undertaken a campaign to get rid of his acne. He shampoos regularly, brushes his teeth twice a day, and has made flossing a habit.

One of Mark's first steps was to get rid of his old and tattered clothes. He asked his parents to help in choosing appropriate styles, and he is also beginning to show good judgment of his own.

With the advice of his physician, Mark has begun to exercise regularly. He has started a program of walking to lose weight. Mark has to admit that he feels better already. Although he has not yet taken up sports, he would like to play football when he is in condition.

The physician has also given Mark a weight-loss diet. With his parents' help, he is sticking to it and has already shed a few pounds. He hasn't given up his love for junk food, but he is limiting his consumption. He is trying to avoid too much caffeine, too.

One of the highlights of Mark's turnaround is that he has gotten to know the school counselor, Jack Thomas. Mr. Thomas provides support and encouragement. Mark likes him very much and sees him as a role model.

With all this, Mark's self-esteem is rising rapidly. He is showing more self-control, consideration for others, and assertiveness with his peers. He is also dealing better with his parents' divorce.

As his academic work has improved, Mark gets along better in school. Other students are becoming friendlier, and Mark has even made a couple of close buddies.

Mark has not completely reached his goal, but he is making excellent progress. If you have any of his worries, what you have read in this book should help you get on the road to better health, higher self-esteem, and a happier you.

GLOSSARY
EXPLAINING NEW WORDS

acceptance Approval; favorable reception by one's peers.

acne A skin disorder that causes pimples on the face.

anorexia nervosa/bulimia Two eating disorders affecting persons who have an unrealistic fear of becoming fat.

commitment An act of pledging or promising oneself to a course of action.

cuticle The skin around the fingernail bed.

dental floss A nylon thread used to remove food particles that a toothbrush may miss.

dermatologist A doctor who specializes in treating skin disorders.

endorphins Chemical substances released in the body that reduce stress and promote good feeling.

halitosis Unpleasant or bad-smelling breath.

hygiene Practices that promote health, such as cleanliness.

negative Unfavorable; expressing denial.

plaque A sticky film formed on tooth surfaces that can lead to decay.

positive Expressing approval; stressing the good.

role model A person whose behavior is considered worthy of being copied.

FOR FURTHER READING

Glassman, Bruce S. *Growing Up Male.* New York: The Rosen Publishing Group, 1991.

Madaras, Linda. *The What's Happening to My Body? Book for Boys.* New York: Newmarket Press. 1988.

McCoy, Kathy. *Changes and Choices: A Junior High Survival Guide.* New York: The Putnam Publishing Group, 1989.

McFarland, Rhoda. *Coping Through Self-Esteem.* New York: The Rosen Publishing Group, 1993.

Prudden, Bonnie. *Teenage Fitness.* Cleveland: World Almanac Education, 1988.

INDEX

About the Author

Bruce McGlothlin is a school psychologist/counselor employed by the Allegheny Intermediate Unit in Pittsburgh, Pennsylvania. He holds graduate degrees in both school psychology and counseling. He is the author of *Traveling Light*, a self-exploration guide for adolescents.

Bruce and his wife, Judi, are the parents of two teenage children, Michael and Molly. His hobbies include ultra-marathon running, reading, and jigsaw puzzles.

Photo Credits
All photos on cover and in book by Stuart Rabinowitz.

Design & Production: Blackbirch Graphics, Inc.